Roanoke

ROANOKE

The Story of
THE LOST COLONY

BY PETER I. BOSCO

Spotlight on American History
The Millbrook Press • Brookfield, Connecticut

Cover illustration from *America 1585: The Complete Drawings of John White*, by Paul Hulton. © 1984 The University of North Carolina Press. Color plates © The British Museum. Used by permission. Photographs and illustrations courtesy of: Culver Pictures, Inc.: p. 13; National Portrait Gallery, London: pp. 17, 18, 49, 53; Library of Congress: pp. 23, 27, 43, 59; from *America 1585: The Complete Drawings of John White*, by Paul Hulton. © 1984 The University of North Carolina Press. Color plates © The British Museum. Reprinted by permission; New York Public Library, Arents Collection: p. 51; National Maritime Museum, London: p. 62. Map by Joe Le Monnier.

Library of Congress Cataloging-in-Publication Data
Bosco, Peter I.
Roanoke : the story of the lost colony / by Peter I. Bosco.
p. cm.—(Spotlight on American history)
Includes bibliographical references and index.
Summary: Reviews the events surrounding the founding and mysterious disappearance of the first English settlement in the New World.
ISBN 1-56294-111-9
1. Roanoke Colony (N.C.)—Juvenile literature.   [1. Roanoke Colony (N.C.)]   I. Title.   II. Series.
F229.B74 1992   975.6′175—dc20   91-19887 CIP AC

Contents

for my goddaughter
Sophia Van Valkenburg

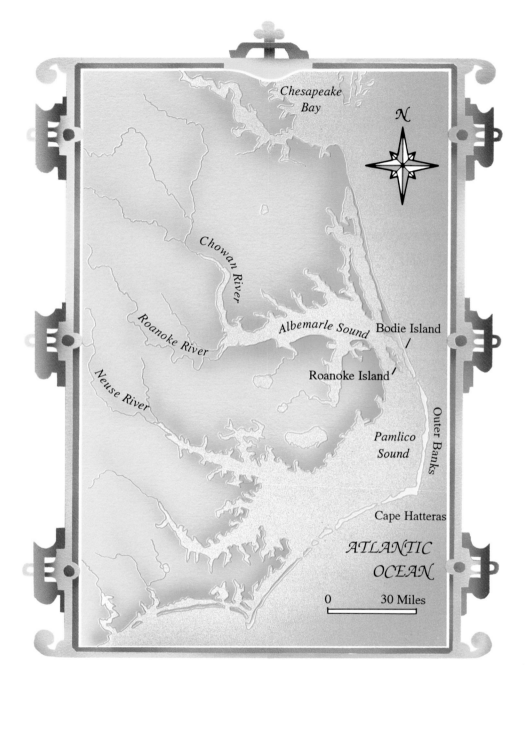

1

WHITE RETURNS

Four months and thousands of nautical miles had passed since the warship *Hopewell* set sail from Plymouth, England. Having finished her mission in the Caribbean, she at last sighted the shores of North America in August 1590.

John White breathed a sigh of relief. His long journey would soon be at an end. In his journal that evening White wrote thankfully: "We are within three leagues of the low sandy islands west of Wococon."

Wococon (a name no longer used) was part of a chain of windswept barrier islands known today as the Outer Banks. These narrow little islands, now part of the state of North Carolina, are hardly more than sandbars.

Between the Outer Banks and the mainland were two huge but very shallow sounds. Between the two sounds lay John White's destination—an island called Roanoke. It was there, three years earlier, that John White had left a struggling group of English colonists. A member of the colony, he had sailed back to England, promising to return the following spring with more supplies and settlers.

But fate had other plans for John White and the Roanoke colony. Because of events beyond his control, White did not return that spring. Nor did he return the next spring. In fact, in the three years since White's departure, no English ship had been able to visit the colony.

As the *Hopewell* began to work its way up the Outer Banks, a sudden hurricane struck. Fierce winds blew the English ship out to sea. For five days the turbulent waters tossed the vessel about like a toy.

When the storm finally broke, the crew again sighted land. It was the small barrier islands west of Wococon. They were back where they had started six days earlier!

Some crew members believed that the storm was a bad omen. They urged that the mission be abandoned and the *Hopewell* return directly to England. But, pressured by White, the captain of the *Hopewell* continued.

Three days later, the *Hopewell* reached Croatoan Island, near present-day Cape Hatteras, about forty miles south of Roanoke Island. White was well acquainted with the tiny Indian tribe that lived on Croatoan. They had always been friendly to the English. His eyes searched the shoreline, hoping to see a band of natives waving excitedly at the slowly passing English ship. But he saw only sand and forested dunes. There was no sign of life.

Three days after that, the *Hopewell* dropped anchor opposite the inlet that led to Roanoke Sound. This was as far as the *Hope-*

well could go. The inlet and the sound beyond were much too shallow for the warship to enter. The rest of the journey had to be made in rowboats.

The next day John White set out with a search party in two boats. Behind them the *Hopewell's* heavy cannons roared to alert the colonists that the English had returned. After stopping on a small barrier island to refill empty water casks, the two boats rowed across the inlet. Strong winds churned up huge waves and made the going very rough. One boat capsized. The sailors tried in vain to cling to the overturned boat, but they were swept away. Only the four best swimmers managed to survive. Seven others, including the captain of the *Hopewell,* disappeared forever beneath the violent surf.

The sight of this sudden tragedy so upset the crew of the other boat that, as White recorded later, the men "were all of a mind not to go any further to seek the colonists." In the moment of crisis that followed, he convinced the others to press on.

John White's will to continue came not just from a simple promise to the colonists that he would return. He had more at stake than that. White had not been happy about leaving the colony in the first place. He had hoped it would be his home for the rest of his life. Most of his belongings were there. More important, when he had departed three years earlier, he had left family behind—his daughter, his son-in-law, and his week-old grandchild. The infant was Virginia Dare, the first English child to be born in the New World.

Night fell as the boat moved up Roanoke Sound. In the dark, it overshot the landing point. The party was about to turn around when the sailors spotted a large fire at the northern end of the island. A signal from the colonists at last, thought White. A trumpet blast from the boat split the night air. There was no reply. The sailors then called out and sang familiar English songs, but there was still no response from the shore.

The party spent the night in the boat. At dawn they landed where the fire had been. They found, however, that it had only been a brush fire, possibly caused by lightning.

From there, White and the search party continued on foot to the place where the colony had been. Along the way they found footprints, but these appeared to be the tracks of bare Indian feet, not of boot-shod Englishmen.

So far there had been no sign of the colonists—no sounds, no signals. As he got closer to the place where he had left his colony in 1587, White grew more and more nervous about what he might find. Before he had left, there had been friction between the colonists and the local Indians. He began to think that his worst fear might be true. Could the Indians have attacked and destroyed the colony?

When the party at last reached the settlement, John White found more questions than answers. Not a soul was around. Yet neither were any dead bodies, nor even a skeleton. The fort was undamaged. In fact, nothing suggested that there had been any sort of struggle here.

However, the houses where the colonists had lived had all been neatly removed. This made sense to White because the planks, panels, floorboards, bolts, locks, hinges, tiles, doors, windows, and furniture would have been needed for new homes elsewhere.

Could the colonists have been forced to leave? If so, they surely would have carved a cross someplace (as White had instructed them to do before he left) to show that they were in some sort of trouble. If they were in trouble, would they have had time to take apart their houses?

The only clue left by the Roanoke settlers was
the word CROATOAN, *carved on a tree.*

The colonists had also taken the time to bury carefully three large chests containing White's belongings. It appeared that some Indians had later found and looted the chests, for White found strewn "about the place, many of my things, spoiled and broken and my books torn from their covers . . . some of my pictures and maps rotten and spoiled with rain, and my armor almost eaten through with rust."

But where had the more than one hundred colonists gone? White found a single, tantalizing clue. "One of the chief trees . . . had the bark taken off and five feet from the ground in fair capital letters was graven CROATOAN without any cross or any sign of dis-

[13]

tress." Could that be it? Had the colonists moved to Croatoan Island? Before White left in 1587, there had been much talk of moving the settlement. Several places were suggested, but never Croatoan. There was no harbor there, no place where ships could anchor safely. Besides, Croatoan was a small island, surely too small to accommodate so many extra people.

And why, if indeed the colony had gone there, had no one tried to signal the *Hopewell* when she had passed Croatoan a few days earlier? White wished he had made an immediate search of the island. There was no choice but to return to Croatoan and get some answers.

One thing was certain, however. England's dream of colonizing North America was not off to a good start. Her only colony had vanished, almost without a trace.

What went wrong at Roanoke? How did the English lose touch with their lone colony for so long? Who were these missing colonists? Why had they come to America? And where could they have gone?

To answer these questions, it is necessary to look back to the very beginning of the Roanoke story.

2

A NEW WORLD

In 1492, Christopher Columbus set sail across the Atlantic Ocean. On the other side of this huge body of water he found a landmass so vast that it would be called the New World.

The New World, however, was not to be shared equally among the countries of the Old World. Columbus had claimed the Americas for Spain, and the Spaniards were determined to keep these lands for themselves.

Along the wild shoreline of these new continents, Spain built many outposts and military bases. The conquistadors Hernando Cortés and Francisco Pizarro marched Spanish armies deep into the untamed interior to conquer the rich Aztec and Inca empires. Spain's treasury soon overflowed with plundered gold and silver.

Spain was becoming the mightiest nation on earth. Tiny England, on the other hand, was still a weak and backward country.

She had not yet begun her reign as the world's greatest naval power. And, by the late 1500s, many Englishmen had begun to argue that, unless England started building an overseas empire of her own, she would never take her rightful place among the great nations of Europe.

*E*NGLAND'S RULER, Queen Elizabeth I, was eventually persuaded to colonize the New World. Elizabeth had become a bitter enemy of the Spanish king, Philip II. She liked the idea of an English colony in America in part because she knew it would be a thorn in King Philip's side.

In June 1578 the queen granted one of her court noblemen, Sir Humphrey Gilbert, permission to establish a colony in North America. That November, Gilbert set sail with ten ships and five hundred men to explore the coast of North America in preparation for planting a colony.

Things went badly from the start. The captains of four of Gilbert's ships decided to abandon the mission and become pirates. Several others soon had to turn back because they did not have enough food and supplies. Gilbert's remaining ships were scattered in a November storm and forced to seek safety in English ports.

Only one ship, the *Falcon*, pressed on. Her captain was Gilbert's twenty-four-year-old half-brother, Walter Raleigh. He sailed the *Falcon* down the Atlantic as far south as the Cape Verde Islands, off the coast of Africa. There the English ship ran into a superior Spanish force. Not one to run from a fight, Captain Raleigh faced the Spanish but was soon forced to break off the battle.

The *Falcon* limped home, reaching England late in May 1579. Colonizing America was more involved and difficult than the En-

Queen Elizabeth I.
She is shown standing
on a map of England.

Sir Walter Raleigh. In this portrait, he is pictured with his son.

glish had imagined. The first attempt was a disaster. Walter Raleigh was disappointed, but he would not yet admit defeat.

The following year, Raleigh was sent to Ireland as a captain of the infantry to help put down a revolt against English rule. There he demonstrated his keen ability as a soldier and as an administrator. He returned to England in 1581.

Back at the queen's court, he was known for his style and wit. Muscular, slender, and over six feet tall, Raleigh was gifted with both good looks and great charm. It wasn't long before he won the queen's favor. The story goes that Raleigh caught Queen Elizabeth's attention when he spread his best plush cloak over a puddle before her, so that she would not get her feet wet as she walked over it. If this really happened, then the loss of his cloak was repaid many times over by the rewards she gave him as the years went on.

By 1583, Raleigh and Gilbert were ready to try again to establish a colony in America. The queen, however, would not permit Raleigh to go on such a hazardous expedition. So, Sir Humphrey sailed without him. Gilbert reached Newfoundland before foul weather forced the small fleet back to England. On the return voyage Gilbert and his flagship were caught in a fierce Atlantic gale and swallowed up by the sea.

STILL DETERMINED to colonize the New World, Raleigh sent two ships the following April to find a suitable place. On July 4, 1584, after sixty-nine days at sea, the crew sighted the coast of North America. The following week they landed on one of the islands that form the Outer Banks. The exact location of their landfall is not known. It was probably near Nags Head on Bodie Island (about five miles from Kitty Hawk, where the Wright brothers would make their historic first flight 319 years later).

For two days the English explored the narrow strip of land. It was full of wild grapes, which gave a sweet smell to the hot summer breeze. The sailors picked the grapes and ate them in the shade of bushy red cedar trees. There were flocks of seagulls, which could be seen snatching up large clams in their beaks and dropping them on the rocks to break them open.

Except for the small animals and deer that roamed about freely, the little green island appeared to be deserted. The English, however, were being closely watched from the woods.

Not far from where the two English ships were anchored lived a tribe of Algonquian-speaking Indians called the Roanokes. They were one of the many groups of woodland Indians that lived in most of what is now the eastern United States, from New England to the Carolinas. The languages of these groups sprang from the same basic stock, but each group spoke its own dialect.

These Indians were a proud people with a complex and interesting culture. Their civilization had been in existence for about 1,500 years when Walter Raleigh's two ships arrived in 1584. Yet their world would soon change dramatically.

The Roanokes had a sophisticated culture, but no written language with which to pass down their knowledge. They knew nothing of iron, or even the wheel. Imagine the wonder and excitement that must have stirred the Roanoke villages when word was brought of the strange ships lying off the coast.

3

RALEIGH'S VIRGINIA

For two days the English had been anchored off Bodie Island. On the third day they saw a lone Indian walking along the beach opposite the ships. Several Englishmen rowed out to make their first encounter with a Native American. According to their account: "After he had spoken of many things not understood by us, we brought him with his own good liking, aboard the ships, and gave him a shirt, a hat, and some other things."

After getting a tour of the ship the Indian left. He then gathered a bounty of fish to repay the English: "In less than half an hour, he had laden his boat as deep as it could swim . . . After he had requited the former benefits received, he departed out of our sight."

It must have taken iron nerve for that single Indian to go aboard that ship, but it was surely a fantastic moment for him. To someone used to a world of forest trails and simple villages, everything on board would be completely new. He had worn only animal skins his whole life, so the fine linen shirt he was given must have been quite a wonder to him.

*T*HE RULER of the Roanokes was a king named Wingina (which means Complacent One). Most of his people lived on the mainland in a village called Dasemunkepeuc. Part of the tribe lived under the rule of the king's brother, Granganimeo (He Restrains from Ridicule), on Roanoke Island, which lies midway between the mainland and Bodie Island.

Over the next few weeks, the Roanokes began to trade with the English. Metal objects were of particular interest to the Indians. Twenty deer skins were traded for a tin plate, and fifty for a copper kettle. King Wingina, who had suffered a severe battle wound, could not attend these meetings with the English. He sent Granganimeo as his official representative.

Granganimeo visited the English aboard their ships and sampled his first bread and wine. Later, he even brought his wife and children aboard the ship—an extraordinary sign of trust. "They had our ships in marvelous admiration," wrote the admiral in his log, "as it appeared that none of them had ever seen the like."

Eventually a party of Englishmen went to Granganimeo's village on Roanoke Island. Probably no more than forty-five people lived on the island, which was just three miles wide and twelve miles long. Their village consisted of nine rectangular huts and was surrounded by a palisade, or fence of sharpened wooden poles. Although surprised by the unexpected visit, Granganimeo's wife proved to be a most gracious hostess. She bid the Englishmen:

*Members of
the expedition
sent by Raleigh
trade with
the Roanokes.*

Sit down by a great fire, and after took off our clothes, and washed them and dried them again. Some of the women pulled off our stockings and . . . washed our feet in warm water, and she herself [Granganimeo's wife] took great pains to see all things ordered in the best manner she could making great haste to dress some meat for us to eat.

Wingina kept close watch over the newcomers. Of particular interest to the king were the Englishmen's armor, their swords, and especially their guns, which produced sounds like thunder and could kill at great distances.

The Roanokes had recently been at war with two neighboring tribes. In the fighting King Wingina's thigh was pierced clean through by an arrow. Wingina was not sure who the English were, but it is clear that he wished to enlist their help against his enemies. He would invite the English to stay on Roanoke Island when they returned the next year with colonists.

FINALLY, AFTER being anchored off Bodie Island for five weeks, the English set sail for home. Besides many colorful stories about the Indians, they brought back two men. One was a Roanoke named Wanchese (which means, very appropriately, He Who Flies Out). The other, named Manteo (He Snatches from an Eagle), was not from Roanoke but from Croatoan Island.

In mid-September the expedition reached England and presented Raleigh with a glowing report of the land they said the natives called Wingandacoia. (This name was widely publicized for a time. Later, however, it was found that the Indians had not understood the English when asked the name of their country. At the time an Indian had casually commented, "Wingan-da-acoia," which merely meant "You wear good clothes.")

The report made the new land sound like a Garden of Eden: "The earth bringeth forth all things in abundance, as in the first creation, without toil or labor. The soil is the most plentiful, sweet, fruitful, and wholesome of all the world."

The English had found the greenery of the Outer Banks to be breathtaking. Yet the lushness of the islands concealed the fact that the sandy soil there was not very good for most farming. Moreover, the expedition had seen this area at its best, in late summer, when the weather was most pleasant.

Worst of all, because of the shallowness of the sounds, there were no natural harbors for large vessels. Most ships would have to anchor off the coast, where they would be in danger from coastal storms. The English did not yet know that the Carolina coastline was, and still is, subject to violent squalls that blow in without warning. (The Outer Banks would later get the nickname "Graveyard of the Atlantic" because so many ships were lost there.)

Not having seen the area himself, Raleigh was content with the reports. He was convinced that Roanoke Island would be an ideal spot for the first English settlement in America. By the spring of 1585, preparations for a colony were well under way. Raleigh decided to call the new territory Virginia in honor of Elizabeth, the Virgin Queen of England. She, in turn, knighted him, and he became Sir Walter Raleigh.

THROUGHOUT MARCH of 1585 ships were readied and over one hundred men were recruited for the new colony. The tons of supplies necessary for a transatlantic voyage—barrels of salted beef, sacks of flour, kegs of beer, casks of water, crates of sailors' biscuits, and so forth—were hauled on creaking horse carts through narrow cobblestone streets to the piers of English ports.

On April 9, 1585, Good Friday, Raleigh's fleet set sail for America. (Sir Walter, forbidden by the queen to go himself, would in fact never see North America.) Scattered by a storm, the ships arrived at separate times off the Outer Banks between June and July. The main supply ship, which contained essential provisions for the colony, was dashed against the shore by a sudden windstorm. Much of the vital food and equipment she carried was lost in the swirling coastal waters.

While the rest of the fleet made necessary repairs, four small boats were sent to explore what is now called Pamlico Sound, just south of Roanoke Island. There the English visited four villages of the Secotan tribe. At one village, the Indians apparently took a silver cup from the visiting English. When the English returned to reclaim their property, the Indians fled in fear. Unable to find the culprits, the English took an action that seems unnecessarily harsh by today's standards. They burned the deserted village and the surrounding crops.

This brutal English justice shocked the Secotans. Yet it may have been welcome news to the tribe's sworn enemies, the Roanokes. King Wingina probably believed more than ever that he had found a new and powerful ally.

Arrangements were now made, by invitation of Wingina, for the English to settle on Roanoke Island. By the end of September a neat little settlement, consisting of a small fort surrounded by English-style cottages, was taking shape. Because of the earlier loss of supplies, the settlement had to be smaller than planned. Much worse, the colonists would now be dependent on food supplied by

The English arrive at Roanoke in the summer of 1585.

the Indians. This would later become a source of tension between the Roanokes and the newcomers.

There was another concern. The same land that Sir Walter Raleigh called Virginia, the Spanish called Ajacán. Spain's King Philip considered this area to be part of his empire. So far the Spanish knew nothing about the Roanoke colony, but Raleigh knew that sooner or later they would find out about it.

It is not surprising, therefore, that most of the "settlers" were soldiers. There were no women or children—and no farmers. Indeed, the settlement seemed to have been more a military outpost than a colony in the traditional sense. It is unlikely that many of the men expected to spend their lives there.

Nevertheless, Raleigh's dream had been realized. For the first time, a year-round English settlement had been firmly planted on the shores of the New World. In the early fall of 1585 the governor of the colony, Captain Ralph Lane, would proudly title an entry in his log, "From the new fort in Virginia."

4

HARIOT AND
WHITE

The first autumn in America passed smoothly enough. The English traded goods such as metal pots and knives for Indian furs and handicrafts and, above all, for food. Communication between the two groups was much easier than it had been the year before, thanks to the presence of Manteo and Wanchese, the two Indians who had gone to England. They had learned English and taught some of their own language in return.

The colonists also had time to explore their new surroundings. Among other things, the English were looking for sources of gold and silver. They collected rock samples and tested them for precious mineral deposits. But they were repeatedly disappointed—there were simply none to be found in that part of the world.

Luckily for history, there were two men in Raleigh's colony who were more interested in recording what they saw of the world around them than in prospecting for gold or collecting deer skins. One was a scientist named Thomas Hariot. The other man was John White, who was a professional artist. Working closely together, the two partners made an honest and accurate record of the people who lived in the region. In pictures and in words, they provided a detailed, in-depth study of American Indians in their natural environment.

WHITE AND HARIOT'S survey, published in 1588, showed the Carolina Indians living a settled life in small villages of one hundred to two hundred people. Each village contained ten to twenty houses. These houses were made of sheets of tree bark and woven reeds, supported by a framework of poles bent and tied to form a barrel-like roof. There were no windows, but the woven sides could be rolled up to let in more air during the warm months. In cold weather, fires were built inside for heat. The smoke escaped through a roof opening with a movable flap. The only pieces of furniture the Indians had were the wooden benches that they slept on at night.

Next to each village were the Indians' cornfields. One of White's drawings shows an Indian boy squatting above the corn on a small platform supported by wooden stilts and covered with a dome-shaped reed hut. What purpose could such a structure possibly serve? The Indians were clever farmers. To protect their crops from hungry birds, they had developed the scarecrow.

The person assigned to scarecrow duty was someone who was not strong enough to do other work, such as a child or an old person. He or she would hide in the little hut and wait for invading birds. When they came, the scarecrow would spring from the hiding place, waving wildly, and frighten the birds away. Later, these living scarecrows were replaced with cornstalk-stuffed figures.

Their rype cornes

Their greene corne

Corne newly sprong

Their sitting at meate

The house where the Tombe of their Herounds standeth

SECOTON

A Ceremony in their prayers so songes, iestures and songe dansing abovte posts carved on the topps lyke mens faces.

A Secotan village, as painted by John White. At the right are fields of corn in three stages of growth, indicating that the Indians made three plantings a year.

Hariot was much impressed with the Indian cornfields. Unlike the white men who would later tear down vast forests to create fields for planting, the Indians were conservationists. They planted their crops in natural clearings. Hariot also noted with surprise that the Indians could get high yields "with[out] muck, dung or any other thing." One reason for this was that the Indians, unlike European farmers, allowed bean vines to grow free and wild among their corn. Although this puzzled Hariot, it is known today that the bean plants introduced nitrogen to the soil at root level, so that the cornstalks were continually fertilized.

Hariot was impressed with other things the Indians grew. Sunflowers, grown for their seeds and their oil, astounded him with their huge size. He also commented on the medicinal herbs grown by the Indians, to which were attributed many healing qualities.

The Indians, Hariot noted, cultivated a plant they called *uppowoc*. They first dried and ground the *uppowoc* leaves. Then they would "take the fume or smoke thereof by sucking it through pipes made of clay into the stomach and head." He went on to say:

It purgeth [illness and] opens all the pores and passages of the body, by which means the use thereof not only preserveth the body from obstructions, but also . . . bodies are notably preserved in health and know not many grievous diseases wherewithall we in England are oftentimes afflicted.

Uppowoc was the plant *Nicotiana rustica*, or tobacco. Hariot, of course, was wrong about tobacco having medicinal qualities. Yet because he believed that it did, he used it for the rest of his life. Sadly, Thomas Hariot was the first documented case of a smoker who died of cancer.

An Indian woman and baby from a village on the North Carolina mainland, as portrayed by John White. In his description, Hariot noted that children were often carried in this way.

During the growing season, the Indians also gathered a wide variety of edible wild plants. Grapes, walnuts, prickly pears, red mulberry, crabapples, hickory, huckleberries, persimmon, and cranberries grew in plenty along Carolina's eastern shore.

White's watercolor of Indians fishing. Their boats were made by hollowing out logs with fire and sharp seashells.

The Indians were excellent hunters. Unlike many of the Europeans who came later, the Indians used all of the animals they killed. The whitetail deer was an important food source. They also ate black bears, raccoons, and rabbits. Besides eating the meat, the Indians had many uses for the animals' hides, bones, sinews, and organs. Nothing was wasted.

The Indians traded their surplus deer skins and other pelts with the colonists for English goods. However, a thriving fur trade did not develop. The English hoped to establish a fur trade, but the Indians regarded the greed of the Englishmen for furs with great distaste. They killed only as many wild beasts as they needed. They would never slaughter animals just for their hides.

Fishing provided another important food source for the Indians. Hariot and White made a detailed record of the marine life in the Carolina waters that shows a wide variety of fish. While White busily drew many fine pictures of the water creatures they studied, Hariot tasted them. He was, for example, impressed with the size of Carolina's sea turtles, many of which were "a yard in breadth and better." Hariot noted that "their backs and bellies are shelled very thick" but added that "they are very good meat as [are] also their eggs."

The two men also observed what was in the skies. Hariot identified forty-eight birds. The men caught, made pictures of, and ate twenty-three kinds of land birds and waterfowl, including trumpeter swans and bald eagles.

THE MOST SIGNIFICANT portion of White and Hariot's study was its sensitive portrait of Indian life. Unusual for the time, Hariot's writing reveals his deep respect for the native culture he ob-

The Mathematician and The Artist

THOMAS HARIOT (1560–1621) did much in his life to further the cause of science. For example, he made the first map of the moon, using one of the earliest telescopes (an instrument that he had built himself). His most significant contributions were in the field of mathematics.

However, Hariot published almost none of his mathematical work in his lifetime. Instead, he is best remembered for the practical work he did in Virginia as a scientific adviser to Sir Walter Raleigh.

The life of John White is more of a mystery. Even the dates of his birth and death are not known for certain. It is known, however, that White accompanied a 1577 expedition to the Arctic. There he drew scenes of Eskimo life in elaborate detail. Like Hariot, John White is remembered most for what he did in Raleigh's Virginia. He was a keen observer of nature and people.

Hariot wrote and White illustrated a *Briefe and True Report on the New Found Land of Virginia*, published in 1588. Hariot's detailed observations with White's watercolors provide a valuable study of Indian life in the sixteenth century.

A common box tortoise, by John White.

served. Hariot admired what he saw as the strong moral and social character of the Indians. He found them to be honest, polite, and generous. They were not obsessed with becoming rich, as the English were. Rather, they seemed content with what they took from the earth.

The Indians ate simple and natural foods and did not overeat, observed Hariot. "They are very sober in their eating and drinking," he wrote, "and consequently very longe lived." Hariot was obviously thinking of the benefits of the Indians' simple diet when he wrote:

> *I would to God we would follow their example. For we should be free from many kinds of diseases which we fall into by sumptuous and unseasonable banquets, continually divising new sauces, and provocation of gluttony to satisfy unsatiable appetite.*

Hariot was fascinated by all aspects of Indian life, from birth to death. He was surprised to find that the Indians' ideas about an afterlife were not much different from his own. He wrote that the Indians believed that when a person dies "the soul is departed from the body." The soul then travels either to Heaven "to enjoy perpetual bliss" or to a place called Popogusso, near the setting sun, to "burn continually in a great pit."

The orderly and closely knit Indian society had long-standing social and religious traditions. Politically, however, it was just beginning to change at about the time the English came. The Indians were moving from small groups, each controlled by a local chieftain, to larger federations that were nearly states in the modern sense. But the course of the Indians' political development was interrupted by the arrival of the Europeans, and it will never be known what those new states would have been like.

While Thomas Hariot wrote, John White was busy with his brush. White's detailed illustrations give historians a valuable picture of how the Carolina Indians looked and dressed. The people in White's colorful pictures wore a dazzling variety of animal hides, headbands, necklaces, bracelets, body paint, feathers, shells, pearls, bear claws, bird talons, and tattoos. Like Hariot, John White did not think of his subjects as savages, but as men and women he had come to admire and respect. The people he drew were tall and straight. In fact, they towered over Englishmen. They were well developed and had strong facial features. Their skin was copper in color. Their hair was black and gleaming. The men shaved their heads, except for a coxcomb of hair down the middle. The women had long hair with short bangs.

The Carolina Indians were a very clean people, too. Unlike Europeans at that time, the Indians washed regularly, bathing in rivers almost every day, even in winter. To them, the Englishmen—with their long hair, beards, and grimy skin—must have appeared very untidy indeed.

5

THE LAST DAYS OF
A ROANOKE KING

While Hariot and White recorded their observations of the new colony, Governor Ralph Lane did some exploring. As he became more familiar with the land and with the shallow waters surrounding Roanoke Island, it became clear to him that the colony's site was not the best place for a permanent settlement. In early November he sent a party of men to explore the area north of the Outer Banks, an area that is now part of the state of Virginia.

There the expedition stumbled upon Chesapeake Bay. This huge bay is home to some of the finest natural deep-water harbors in the world. The explorers visited several villages of the Chesapian tribe. They made close friends with the Chesapians and stayed with them all winter. The English were greatly impressed with the area. They recommended in their report to Governor Lane that he move the colony there as soon as possible.

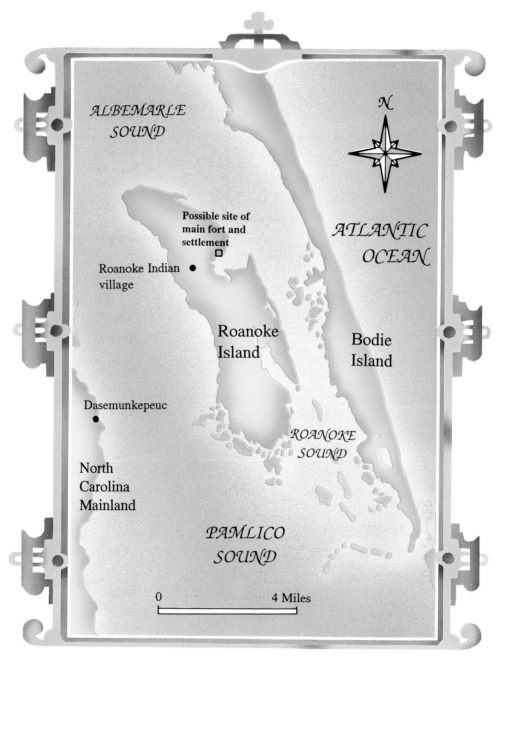

ALBEMARLE
SOUND

N

ATLANTIC
OCEAN

Possible site of
main fort and
settlement

Roanoke Indian
village

Roanoke
Island

Bodie
Island

Dasemunkepeuc

ROANOKE
SOUND

North
Carolina
Mainland

PAMLICO
SOUND

0   4 Miles

Governor Lane was much impressed with the report of the expedition. He was pleased to hear how well the English explorers had been treated by the natives, for by this time relations between the colonists and Indians on Roanoke Island had become tense.

One reason for this was the problem of feeding the colony. Because the English had lost their main supply ship in a storm just as they had arrived, they were heavily dependent on the Indians for food. The colonists, mostly soldiers, knew little about planting crops or making fish traps. Amazingly, they made no effort to learn from the Indians how to farm and fish. But the Roanokes barely got by on what they grew, gathered, and hunted. The sudden arrival of more than a hundred extra people produced a severe strain on the tribe. The stress was greatest during the winter and early spring, when food sources were limited.

As tensions between the two groups increased, Governor Lane did little to ease them. Ralph Lane was a hot-tempered man. A soldier by profession, he tended to resort to the use of force rather than to waste time trying to work things out. His fighting experience was ideal for defending the Roanoke outpost, especially against a Spanish force, but he did not know how to build a new society or to establish a good relationship with the Indians.

Lane had not expected to be so dependent on the natives for food. Not only had the main supply ship been wrecked on the coast, but a supply fleet that was supposed to arrive shortly after the colony was set up never showed. The colonists were now desperately counting on a second supply fleet, which they expected to arrive by Easter.

What the Roanoke colonists didn't know was that England and Spain had gone to war. English ships unlucky enough to be in Spanish ports when the war broke out were promptly seized. Many other English ships were at sea, unaware that their country was at war. Because of this, Raleigh's first supply fleet had been ordered instead to spread the word to English vessels at sea not to go near Spanish waters. Even worse, the war meant that the colony's Easter supply fleet never set sail at all.

RELATIONS BETWEEN the Roanokes and the colonists continued to worsen throughout early spring of 1586, but King Wingina and Governor Lane were still on speaking terms in March. At that time Wingina supposedly told Lane that the nearby Chowan tribe and its great leader Menatonon (He Who Listens Carefully) were planning to attack the English. There is no evidence that the Chowan Indians intended to make war on the English. But, not taking chances, Lane went to the chief Chowan village of Chowanoac with an armed party. Bursting into the village and meeting no resistance, the English seized King Menatonon. Two days later Lane released him, after receiving a ransom (most likely paid in corn) and the king's promise of friendship.

Lane decided to continue from Chowanoac in search of copper mines he had been told lay farther inland. He rowed up the Roanoke River with an armed party and two bull mastiffs—huge English hunting dogs that frightened the Indians.

The expedition expected to be fed and sheltered by the Moratuc people, whose land they were exploring. Instead they found that all the villages were completely deserted and there was no food. Three days upriver, an Indian war party ambushed the expedition. A hail of arrows fell on the English but apparently dropped harmlessly off their steel helmets and body armor. No one was injured.

A nineteenth-century print showing the English at
Roanoke. The settlers depended on the Indians for food,
and this strained relations between the two groups.

Cold, wet, and hungry, Lane and his men faced a long and difficult row back to Roanoke Island. Along the way they had to eat the two dogs to stay alive. They stopped in the land of the Weapemeoc in hope of getting provisions there. Again they found all the villages deserted and all the food taken away.

Lane was convinced that Wingina had set both the Moratuc and the Weapemeoc tribes against him. This very likely was so. The king had by this time become disgusted with his European guests.

*W*INGINA WOULD certainly have been pleased to see Lane and his men perish for another reason. This would prove once and for all that they were mortal and not, as many of the Indians believed, divine beings that could not be destroyed. One view widely held among the Indians, for example, was that the English were dead men who had been allowed to return to earth for a while. Today it is hard to imagine how the Indians could have thought of the English as anything other than ordinary human beings. Yet, from the Indian point of view, the English seemed to possess many supernatural qualities.

Most obviously, there were all their marvelous gadgets—clocks, telescopes, compasses, measuring scales, a foundry, mathematical instruments, and especially guns—which amazed the Indians. They were even more baffled by the Englishmen's seemingly magical ability to send messages by writing.

The Indians also found it strange that there were no women, or children for that matter, among the colonists. In addition, the Englishmen showed no interest in the Indian women. (This, however, was because Lane would not allow his soldiers to show any such interest.)

What puzzled and frightened the Indians most was what they thought was the Englishmen's black magic—an ability to harm individuals from very far away. Even Thomas Hariot noticed that "within a few days after our departure [from a village], the people began to die very fast."

It was not the colonists' magic. It was their germs. Cut off for thousands of years by two great oceans, the peoples of the Americas were never exposed to diseases that were found in Europe. Thus they had not developed resistance to these diseases, as the Europeans had. When the English came to North America, they brought Old World diseases with them. The results were tragic. It has been estimated that ninety percent of the Indian population along the East Coast may have been destroyed by smallpox, measles, tuberculosis, and other European diseases within the first hundred years of colonization.

An Indian wearing body paint and dressed for an important feast. The tail hanging behind helped support a quiver of arrows.

Around Roanoke, Hariot reported that large numbers of people died in each village. And as Indians fled from these epidemics, they spread disease to other areas that had not yet been visited by the English. This convinced the Indians completely that the English had some evil ability to kill their victims from afar.

Whatever the Indians might have believed about the English, it is certain that by early April 1586 the spirit of friendliness that had once existed between the colonists and the Indians on Roanoke Island was completely gone. The colonists' strongest supporter among the Roanokes, Granganimeo, died in March. Wingina's father also died about this time. Wanchese had returned to his own people and was openly hostile to his former hosts. Only Manteo, the Croatoan, was still loyal to the English.

To Wingina's dismay, Lane and his party finally returned from their expedition on Easter Sunday, April 3, hungry but unharmed. And to Ralph Lane's disappointment, Raleigh's promised Easter resupply fleet had not yet arrived.

THE CONSTANT DEMANDS of the colonists on the Roanokes in May—the time of year when food was scarcest—were wearing the Indians out. Finally the pressure on their society became intolerable. King Wingina deserted his village on Roanoke Island and brought all his people over to Dasemunkepeuc on the mainland. There he plotted against the English, for now he feared that they would take violent action.

Indeed, Lane's situation had become life-threatening. With the much-needed Easter supply fleet overdue, he was forced to send about one third of the colonists out in small groups to the barrier islands to live on oysters and wild roots. A smaller colony meant that his position on Roanoke Island was now highly vulnerable to an Indian attack.

Wingina, in fact, was busy making a plan to wipe out the English. He recruited warriors from several neighboring tribal groups, who were to assemble with Wingina and his men at Dasemunkepeuc on the tenth of June. From there the entire war party would cross the sound to Roanoke to attack and overwhelm the colonists.

Lane discovered the plan, however. On the morning of June 1, he went to Dasemunkepeuc with twenty-seven heavily armed men and demanded a meeting with the king. The English entered the village flanked by Wingina's warriors. Only Governor Lane and his bodyguard were allowed to go farther. Armed with a sword and a pistol, he proceeded to the center of the village.

An anxious silence fell as Lane was surrounded by seven or eight of the tribe's leaders. At a distance Lane's soldiers waited tensely. The king stepped forward. Lane was now face-to-face with a man he knew planned to kill him and his colonists.

Suddenly, Lane yelled "Christ our victory"—the prearranged signal to attack. The soldiers fired on the surrounding Indians, then charged. Hit by a pistol ball, Wingina fell to the ground. Then, as if he had never been shot, he sprang to his feet and dashed like a deer from the village. A second ball struck Wingina in the buttocks, but he kept running. Chased by two soldiers, he disappeared into the woods. Lane feared that the king had escaped, but then his men finally emerged from the woods carrying King Wingina's head.

A week later some Englishmen who had been sent to gather oysters on Croatoan Island sighted a great fleet of warships moving up the coast. Was this the supply fleet promised by Raleigh? Or could it be a Spanish squadron sent to destroy the English outpost?

6

THE SECOND ENGLISH
COLONY IN AMERICA

The huge fleet that anchored off the Outer Banks was not the Spanish navy. Nor was it a supply fleet sent by Sir Walter Raleigh. It belonged to Sir Francis Drake, a tough and skillful seaman known as one of England's legendary "sea dogs."

Drake's unexpected visit to the colony was not only a big surprise for Ralph Lane but also a great relief. On June 11 the governor rowed out to meet Sir Francis. Anchored offshore in a neat formation, the fleet must have presented a spectacular and stately sight. Such a large and fine array of fighting ships was not to be seen again in North American waters for many years to come. The two men met aboard Drake's huge flagship. No doubt they had much to talk about.

Sir Francis was surprised to learn that the colony had not yet been resupplied and was falling on hard times. He made Lane a

Sir Francis Drake,
a naval hero in
his own day.

generous offer. Drake would give him enough food, clothing, equipment, and munitions to keep the colony going. He would also leave with Lane skilled craftsmen, oarsmen and boats (to carry out further exploration), and even black slaves. Or, if the governor preferred, Drake would take all the colonists back with him to England.

Lane chose to stay. But just as the supplies were being loaded into the boats for transfer to Roanoke, a tremendous storm broke. Besides thunder, lightning, and heavy rain, there were reportedly "hailstones as big as hens' eggs" and "great spouts [of water] . . . as though heaven and earth would have met." This terrifying storm, the likes of which the colonists had never before seen, lasted three days. Ships blew far out to sea, and several did not return. Many smaller vessels smashed against the barrier islands or capsized.

As governor of England's first settlement in America, Ralph Lane had carried out his mission to the best of his ability. Now, having lost most of the promised supplies in the storm, there was no more he could do. With anguish and disappointment, Lane accepted Drake's offer to evacuate the colony.

Drake's fleet set sail for England on June 18, 1586. Although Ralph Lane was bitter about having to disband the colony, he was very grateful for Drake's timely rescue. Never having received the expected supplies from England, he no doubt felt that Raleigh had abandoned his own colonists.

Sir Walter, however, had not forgotten his colony in the New World. As soon as he had been able, he had sent an emergency supply ship to relieve the colonists. The ship, crew, and cargo were paid for out of Raleigh's own pocket. The ship reached Roanoke before the end of June, perhaps just days after Drake's departure. Finding no colony to relieve, the ship sailed back to England with its supplies.

[50]

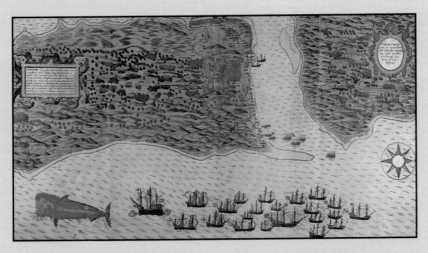

The Sacking of St. Augustine

SIR FRANCIS DRAKE (1540? –1596) was the greatest admiral of the age. In 1580, after three years at sea, Drake became the first Englishman to sail around the world. His voyage was the first circumnavigation of the globe since Ferdinand Magellan's expedition, from 1519 to 1522.

Drake routinely plundered Spanish ports in the New World. One of his last attacks in the New World fell on St. Augustine in Spanish Florida in 1586 (above).

Before Drake torched the town, he ordered his troops to strip the fine Spanish houses of their furniture, windows, and doors. Even the locks and bolts were taken. Drake thought that these things might be useful to the colonists on Roanoke Island.

Raleigh had intended that ship to tide the colony over while he organized the main supply fleet. That fleet, consisting of eight ships under the command of Raleigh's cousin, Sir Richard Grenville, sailed for Virginia in May 1586. Grenville arrived in August with four hundred additional men and a year's supply of food for the colony. He was stunned to find that it had been abandoned.

Grenville decided to leave behind a few soldiers to maintain England's presence in North America. He sent fifteen colonists with a two-year supply of food to reoccupy the settlement. Unaware of the recent conflict with the Roanokes, he could not have known the danger in which he had left his men.

With all the food they needed and no particular tasks, the small group settled in for what they thought would be a pleasant and quiet autumn in America. The remaining Roanokes had other plans for them, however. Wanchese (the one who had gone to England in 1584) was now the leader of the surviving tribe. He and his people were eager to take revenge on the English.

MEANWHILE, BACK IN England, Sir Walter Raleigh watched as his colonists returned, then his relief ship, and then Grenville's fleet. He must have felt frustrated and disappointed. But Raleigh was still not going to give up. Arrangements for another colonizing venture began right away.

Learning from the mistakes of the first colony, the new one would be very different. For one thing, it would have to be located where there was a good harbor, so that ships could anchor safely. It was thus decided that the new settlement would be somewhere along Chesapeake Bay.

But who would be sent? A paid garrison of soldiers would have neither the skills nor the interest to work the land. For the colony

AN° · DÑI · 1571·
ÆTATIS · SVÆ·
·29·

Sir Richard Granville, killed
in a sea-fight near the Azores.
1591

*Sir Richard Grenville,
Raleigh's cousin, led a
relief fleet that reached
Roanoke in 1586.*

to be self-sufficient, it would need farmers, as well as skilled craftsmen. Potential colonists, now called "planters," were offered land in the New World. They were encouraged to take their families.

On May 8, 1587, the planters (including the Croatoan Manteo, who had come back to England with Ralph Lane) left England in three ships, bound for the New World. The governor of the new colony was to be none other than John White. Because he had been part of the earlier attempt to establish a colony, White's presence lent a sense of continuity to the venture. He also set an example of faith, hope, and permanence by bringing along his pregnant daughter, Eleanor, and her husband, a bricklayer named Ananias Dare.

Who were these planters, and where did they come from? Evidence suggests that most, if not all, came from London.

Today it might seem silly to send a group of people accustomed to city life into a wilderness. But in those days London was a city of gardens. Tiny vegetable plots could be found on nearly every block. Many people, even craftsmen, grew at least some of their own food. Moreover, London's swelling population included increasing numbers of farmers who had left the countryside in search of city jobs as unskilled laborers.

The majority of the planters came from the lower middle class. All their names are recorded, but not much is known about their personal backgrounds. Their names are so common that it is almost impossible to trace their family histories.

What is better known is why the planters chose to leave "civilization" for an uncertain life in the wilds of America. Unlike the *Mayflower* Pilgrims of 1620, Raleigh's planters do not seem to have left England in search of religious freedom. There was, however, a general feeling at this time that London had become hopelessly corrupt. The thought of escaping this "city of sin" for a fresh start in a New World almost certainly appealed to many of the planters.

Some of the planters were probably unemployed at the time they were recruited. There were not enough jobs in London for the number of people. Even skilled craftsmen could not work unless they belonged to one of the hard-to-get-into business organizations called trade guilds. It is likely that some of the planters owed large sums of money to moneylenders. For them it might have been wiser to leave the country than to risk being locked away in a debtors' prison.

The possibility of owning land also interested potential colonists. Raleigh promised land to the planters in quantities they could never have acquired in England. White and Hariot assured the planters that farming in North America would be easier than it was in England. The climate was better. Yields per acre were higher. And they could grow a greater variety of crops.

Of course, there would be dangers in the New World. But London could be a dangerous place, too. It was dirty and overcrowded, and it had a high crime rate. Deadly diseases were all too common. It should also be noted that meat was hard to get and very expensive in London. Even fresh fish was not easy to obtain. The prospect of a better diet, including wild game and seafood, was particularly attractive to city dwellers. Reports of good climate, easy farming, plentiful hunting, and free land all served to assure the planters that a better life awaited them in America.

*B*EFORE MAKING FOR Chesapeake Bay, the fleet planned to stop at Roanoke Island to pick up Grenville's caretaker colonists. The long, rough voyage to America was most unpleasant, especially for all the "landlubbing" civilians on board. They were not prepared for the demands of an Atlantic crossing, including cramped living quarters, seasickness and other illness, and the threat of pirate attacks. To make matters worse, Governor White and the admiral of the fleet did not agree on many matters. They were scarcely on speaking terms by the time the ships reached the Outer Banks on July 22, 1587.

White and forty or so of his colonists transferred into a smaller boat to sail into Roanoke Sound and pick up Grenville's men. As soon as the small boat pulled away from the flagship, the admiral yelled down to sailors who manned the boat and ordered them to leave White and the colonists on the island. Later, the remaining planters were also left on Roanoke Island.

It seemed that Raleigh's painstaking efforts to colonize the New World were once again doomed. This time it was because two men, a seaman and a painter, could not get along. The admiral's treachery was a terrible setback for White. Yet he quickly adapted to the sudden turn of events, resolving to make the best of it.

As soon as they landed on Roanoke Island, White and the colonists began looking for Grenville's men. They found instead "the bones of one of those fifteen . . . slain long before." Later, they walked to where the fort had been. There they found deer eating wild melons inside the overgrown, but undamaged, cottages. There was no sign of any Englishmen. Governor White gave up all "hope of ever seeing any of the fifteen men living."

The mystery surrounding the fate of those men must have been chilling for the colonists. Yet there was no more that could be done for them now. Governor White ordered that work begin in earnest to rebuild and reoccupy the old settlement. A new colony soon took shape. The new settlement numbered about 115 planters, including 17 women and 9 children.

So far there were no signs of any Indians. Greatly reduced in number by Ralph Lane's massacre, the remaining Roanokes had gathered at Dasemunkepeuc. On the sixth day, however, a small party of Roanoke warriors hiding among some reeds, possibly deer hunting, saw an Englishman walking along the beach. The planter, George Howe, had foolishly gone out crabbing alone and unarmed. The Indians killed him, then crossed back to the mainland.

Unlike Ralph Lane, who would have called for immediate revenge, Governor White first wanted to be absolutely sure that the Roanokes were responsible for Howe's murder. With Manteo, the governor went to Croatoan Island, Manteo's homeland, to get information on the activities of the Roanokes.

The tiny Croatoan tribe had always been friends of the English, thanks to Manteo, whose mother ruled the island. From the Croatoans, White learned the fate of the fifteen caretaker colonists.

After the attack by the English in which Wingina had been killed, the Roanokes had been looking for revenge. They were anxious to slaughter Grenville's men, but they had only a few warriors left. To their surprise, the Roanokes got help from their enemies, the Secotans (the tribe that had had one of its villages burned to the ground by the English because of a stolen cup).

The Secotans and Roanokes had attacked Grenville's men and killed two of them. The remaining Englishmen, some of them wounded, had managed to make a break for their boats and escape to one of the barrier islands. These thirteen survivors had stayed there a while but then sailed off again, to an unknown destination.

White also learned from the Croatoans that it was indeed Roanoke men who had killed George Howe. John White was a peace-

[57]

ful man by nature, but he must have been pressured by some of the other colonists to punish the Roanokes. The governor reluctantly authorized an attack on Dasemunkepeuc.

At midnight on August 8, with Manteo guiding them, twenty-five men crossed the sound to ambush the unsuspecting Indians. The attack began when the colonists shot an Indian woman in the back. It was not until an Indian cried out the name of one of the soldiers that the English realized the terrible mistake they had made: They had attacked the wrong Indians.

After they had killed George Howe, the terrified Roanokes had deserted their village. They had left behind ripening crops of corn, peas, pumpkins, and tobacco. Soon after, a party of Indians from another tribe went to help themselves to the Roanokes' abandoned crops, with tragic results. These Indians were Croatoans. Poor Manteo had unknowingly led an attack on his own people.

*T*EN DAYS LATER a happier event took place. On August 18, 1587, Governor White's daughter, Eleanor Dare, gave birth to a baby girl. Her parents named the infant Virginia, in honor of their new home. Virginia Dare rightly earned her place in history as the first English child born in America.

The English had little choice but to remain on Roanoke for the winter, but they hoped that in the spring the colony could be moved to Chesapeake Bay as planned. They also decided that one of the colonists should return to England in one of the small vessels that had been used to bring the planters and their gear into the sound. This person would make sure that the expected supply fleet would sail.

No one volunteered. Finally, the colonists decided that the governor himself should go. White refused. He had planned to

A nineteenth-century portrayal of the baptism of Virginia Dare, the first English child born in America.

spend the rest of his life in America. Besides, he argued, it wouldn't be proper for a governor to leave his own colony. But, after days of debate, he finally agreed to return to England.

The planters told the governor that they would leave a message for him should they move to Chesapeake Bay while he was gone. If they were in any danger at that time, they would leave behind the sign of the cross as a distress signal.

On the day he left, John White probably kissed his nine-day-old granddaughter good-bye. He did not know that he would never see her again.

7

AN AMERICAN MYSTERY

Governor White's long, treacherous voyage back to England in the small boat was a nightmare. It is a wonder that he made it alive. As soon as he got back, he urged Raleigh to send supplies to the colony as soon as possible. Raleigh arranged to have a relief fleet sent in the spring.

By the end of March 1588, the ships were ready to sail. At the last minute, however, Queen Elizabeth ordered Raleigh's fleet to military duty. Elizabeth had received reports that her arch rival, King Philip II of Spain, was pulling together a massive naval force to invade England. Known as the Spanish Armada, the huge fleet of some 124 ships would include 8,000 seamen and nearly 20,000 specially trained invasion troops.

The queen put an emergency ban on transatlantic travel. Despite this, Raleigh arranged to have two small vessels sneak out of port on April 22. With White and a few more planters—seven men and four women—the two ships were Virginia bound.

They never made it. Overtaken by French pirates, they were caught in a ferocious sea fight. John White was severely wounded—hit twice in the head, stabbed with a pike, and finally shot. The ships turned back.

In England, White's health recovered, but his spirit must have been crushed by the failure of the mission. Meanwhile an attack by the Spanish Armada appeared to be imminent. White must have wondered if a ship would ever reach his colony.

One did, on May 28. But it was a Spanish ship. The governor of Florida, a Spanish colony, had sent a ship from St. Augustine to Chesapeake Bay—the most logical place for a naval base—to look for an English outpost he believed was there. Not finding anything, the Spanish ship turned around to go back to St. Augustine. Along the Outer Banks, however, the ship was caught in a sudden storm and forced to take shelter in Roanoke Sound.

There the Spanish found a small loading dock, along with some English casks and other debris. Satisfied that they had found the general location of the enemy, the Spanish returned to Florida with their report. Fortunately, because so many Spanish fighting vessels had been sent to join the Armada, the governor did not have enough ships and men available to launch an attack against the English intruders.

In July 1588 the great Armada entered the English Channel, where an English fleet of 197 ships and 16,000 men was waiting. The English nation held its breath. In the great battle that followed, England's navy soundly defeated the Armada. It was the dramatic climax of King Philip's war against the English and a blow from which Spain would never fully recover.

The Spanish Armada battling the English fleet in 1588.

With the threat of a Spanish invasion over, it looked as if John White would at last be able to return to Virginia. By this time, however, Raleigh had lost much of his earlier interest in colonizing North America. The attempts so far had been stressful and profitless. Moreover, his time, energy, and resources were now tied up in other projects.

*W*HITE FINALLY did get passage back to the New World in 1590, aboard the warship *Hopewell*. The *Hopewell*'s primary mission was to make pirate-like raids on Spanish shipping in the Caribbean. For four months, White was no more than a passenger while the ship did its work. It was not until the *Hopewell* entered the Straits of Florida on July 28 that he began to believe that he might see the colony again.

As the *Hopewell* moved up the coast, she was delayed by a hurricane. As White described it: "We had very foul weather with much rain, thundering and a great spouts, which fell round about us nigh unto our ships." The *Hopewell* somehow managed to survive the storm, and it finally dropped anchor off the inlet that led to Roanoke Sound. From there White and a search party continued in rowboats, reaching the site of the colony on August 18, 1590, Virginia Dare's third birthday.

After finding the strange carving of the word CROATOAN, White returned to the *Hopewell*. He convinced the skipper to take him back to Croatoan Island to make a search. But just as they were getting ready to go, a strong storm blew in. It was a close call for the English vessel. With good seamanship and a lot of luck, the captain was just able to pull his ship through. However, approaching the coast again would be too risky. There was no choice but to return to England.

And that was the last John White ever saw of America.

$\mathcal{M}$ORE THAN FOUR CENTURIES have passed since White found the colony abandoned. Over the years many scholars have tried to solve the mystery of the colonists' fate. No one will ever know for sure what became of these English settlers. There is, however, one theory that has gained wide acceptance.

Professor David B. Quinn, a leading authority on the Roanoke colonies, has suggested that most of the colony eventually moved north to Chesapeake Bay, probably in 1588. There the majority of the colonists settled and were gradually absorbed into the Chesapian Indian tribe.

Meanwhile, a small group remained at Roanoke with Manteo to wait for Governor White to return. Perhaps for their protection, Manteo may have taken them to his homeland, Croatoan. (The Croatoans' small island had very limited resources. It would have been able to support a few extra people, but not, as many have thought the case to be, more than one hundred colonists.)

Among the Chesapians, the colonists may have lived peacefully, adapting to their new home. Gradually they could have intermarried with the tribe, becoming more and more "Indianized" each year.

This theory agrees with local Indian traditions. It also fits with another bit of history. On April 26, 1607, an English ship entered Chesapeake Bay with 144 settlers aboard. They founded a new Virginia colony, called Jamestown. In the following days the colonists could see "great smokes of fire" in the distance. The English were unaware of what was going on around them. Later they discovered, with horror, what had happened.

Much of the area around Chesapeake Bay was controlled by a powerful confederacy made up of thirty-two Algonquian-speaking tribes. Its leader, the mighty Powhatan, ruled at least two hundred villages, with a total population of perhaps nine thousand people.

The great chief knew about the people from across the sea who had made their home among the neighboring Chesapians. For nearly twenty years he seems to have considered these foreigners to be harmless enough. However, when more Europeans arrived in 1607, Powhatan felt the need to destroy any potential enemies.

One spring morning Powhatan's warriors attacked the hopelessly outnumbered Chesapians. They burned their villages and killed the inhabitants. None were spared. The entire Chesapian tribe was wiped out—and, if the theory is correct, so were Sir Walter Raleigh's colonists.

By then, however, the lost colonists were already a legend. For generations people have speculated about those daring men and women—the first English people to make America their home. The story of the lost colony will endure, to capture imaginations for years to come, as one of the greatest mysteries in American history.

Chronology

1584	July– August	Two ships sent by Sir Walter Raleigh visit the Outer Banks of North Carolina for five weeks.
1585	April 9	Colony fleet sets sail from England.
	June 26	Essential provisions are lost when the fleet's main supply ship runs aground in bad weather.
	July 16	The English burn a Secotan village to the ground in a dispute over a stolen silver cup.
	July– September	The first English colony in America is established on Roanoke Island.
1586	June 1	King Wingina is killed in Governor Ralph Lane's surprise attack on Dasemunkepeuc.

	June 16–18	Colonists decide to return to England with Sir Francis Drake.
	August	Sir Richard Grenville arrives to find the colony gone. He leaves behind fifteen "caretaker" colonists, who are never heard from again.
1587	May 8	Planters set sail from Plymouth, England, to set up a new colony along Chesapeake Bay.
	July 22	The admiral of the fleet disobeys Raleigh's instructions and leaves the colonists on Roanoke.
	August 18	Virginia Dare is born.
	August 27	Governor John White leaves for England to arrange for a supply fleet for the colony.
1588	Late March	Raleigh's relief fleet, ready to sail, is ordered not to go because of the Spanish Armada crisis.
	April 22	John White manages to sail for Virginia in two small ships with eleven more colonists, but they are forced to return to England after a pirate attack.
1590	March 20	White finally sails for America, aboard the warship *Hopewell*.
	August 18	White and his search party find the settlement abandoned.

Sources

This book would not have come about without the scholarly efforts of four authors whose works were indispensable to my research. Very helpful was *Ralegh's Lost Colony* (Atheneum, 1981), by David Durant, a well-researched book that is thoroughly enjoyable reading. *Roanoke: The Abandoned Colony* (Rowman & Allenheld, 1984), by Karen Kupperman, gives fewer details about the colonies but offers more historical depth and an analysis of sixteenth-century life. David Stick, a native of the Outer Banks, wrote *Roanoke Island: The Beginnings of English America* (University of North Carolina Press, 1983). Somewhat less academic than the others, this is a well-written and highly readable book.

For serious research on this subject one must consult the works of David B. Quinn, who has devoted his life to writing about this topic. Among his works is the definitive two-volume *Roanoke Voyages* (Kraus, 1955), which was used as a resource by every other author I encountered. For my work, I have also relied on Quinn's most recent work, *Set Fair for Roanoke* (University of North Carolina Press, 1985), to resolve any ambiguities or differences among the other authors.

Further Reading

Anderson, David. *The Spanish Armada*. New York: Hampstead Press, 1988.

Buckmaster, Henrietta. *Walter Raleigh: Man of Two Worlds*. New York: Random House, 1964.

Campbell, Elizabeth. *The Carving on the Tree*. Boston: Little, Brown and Co., 1968.

Johnson, Adrian. *America Explored*. New York: Viking Press, 1974.

Lacy, Dan. *The Lost Colony*. New York: Franklin Watts, 1972.

Nee, Kay Bonner. *Powhatan*. Minneapolis: Dillon Press, 1971.

Norman, Charles. *The Shepherd of the Ocean: Sir Walter Raleigh*. New York: David McKay Co., 1952.

Porter, Charles W. *Adventures to a New World: The Roanoke Colony 1585–87*. Washington, D.C.: U.S. Department of the Interior, National Parks Service Office of Publications, 1972.

Index